WHAT THE CHRISTIAN HOPES FOR IN SOCIETY

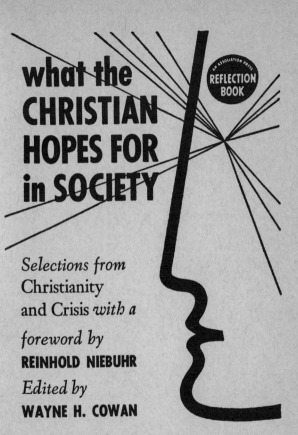

what the CHRISTIAN HOPES FOR in SOCIETY

AN ASSOCIATION PRESS
REFLECTION BOOK

Selections from
Christianity
and Crisis *with a*

foreword by
REINHOLD NIEBUHR

Edited by
WAYNE H. COWAN

Association Press • New York

WHAT THE CHRISTIAN HOPES FOR IN SOCIETY

Price, 50 cents

Library of Congress catalog card number 57-11610

Printed in the United States of America

CONTENTS

FOREWORD

These essays originally appeared in *Christianity and Crisis,* a Christian journal of opinion, which was founded just prior to World War II during the isolationist-interventionist controversy. It was founded by a group of Protestants who challenged the pacifist, neutralist, and isolationist tendencies both in the church and in the nation. The founders believed that the Christian faith is compatible with social and political responsibility which Christians face on every level of human community. They thought that Christian perfectionism was clearly untenable and that it was the responsibility of Christians not to flee, but to come to terms with all the perplexing issues of man's community. This collection of essays represents a cross section of the interests which have been maintained by the editors and readers of the journal as they have sought a Christian perspective on society through these decades in which American power and responsibility have grown so tremendously.

REINHOLD NIEBUHR

ABOUT THE AUTHORS

Now Dean of Union Theological Seminary, JOHN C. BENNETT has been concerned for many years with the relation of Christian faith to the world in which men live and act. This concern is reflected in the titles of a number of his books, which include: *Christianity and Communism, Christian Ethics and Social Policy, The Christian as Citizen, Social Salvation*, and others. Dr. Bennett is Co-Chairman of the Editorial Board of *Christianity and Crisis*. His article, "What Can We Hope for in Society?" originally appeared in January, 1953.

FRANCIS PICKENS MILLER has been involved in practical politics for many years. He has been a candidate for the governorship of Virginia and a candidate for the United States Senate from Virginia. He has long been active as a lay leader in the Christian church, having been involved in various phases of the work of the World Council of Churches and having formerly been president of the World Student Christian Federation. "Christian Faith and Practical Politics" was published in June, 1952.

In protest against Hitler's policies, PAUL TILLICH left Nazi Germany and came to the United States over twenty years ago to teach at Union Seminary in New York City. He is now University Professor at Harvard University. Someone has said, "What Alfred N. Whitehead is to American philosophy, Paul Tillich is to American theology." Dr. Tillich is one of the most perceptive and persuasive interpreters of Christian faith to modern man. "Religion and Its Intellectual Critics" first appeared in March, 1955.

DAVID E. ROBERTS' untimely death at the early age of 44 deprived the Christian community of one of its ablest young interpreters. His pioneering work in the relation of Christian faith to psychotherapy and the church's concern with mental health is of note as is his work in the Christian significance of existentialism, part of which is preserved in his book, published posthumously, *Existentialism and Religious Belief.* His contribution to this collection, "The Christian Gospel and the American Way of Life," appeared in March, 1952.

As an outstanding anthropologist, MARGARET MEAD has lectured widely and has written numerous books, the latest being *New Lives for Old.* Dr. Mead is Associate Curator of Ethnology at the American Museum of Natural History and is Adjunct Professor of Anthropology at Columbia University. "Christian Faith and Technical Assistance" was printed in January, 1955.

AMOS N. WILDER is a New Testament scholar and is at present a professor at Harvard Divinity School, but he has maintained through the years a sensitivity to the arts and particularly to poetry. Being a writer of poetry, Dr. Wilder has written with perception such books as *Spiritual Aspects of the New Poetry* and *Modern Poetry and the Christian Tradition*. His concern that the church gain appreciation of the modern arts has involved him in the work of the Department of Worship and the Arts, of the National Council of Churches. His essay "Artist and Believer" appeared in October, 1953.

KENNETH W. THOMPSON is Assistant Director for the Social Sciences at the Rockefeller Foundation. Dr. Thompson, who gave the 1957 Riverside Lectures at Riverside Church in New York City, under the title, "Philosophy and Practice in American Foreign Policy: A Protestant Realist Critique," has written a number of articles for such journals as *World Politics* and the *Political Science Quarterly*.

A former Northwestern University professor, he grapples unceasingly with such problems as those raised in "Prophets and Politics," which appeared in May, 1955.

The founding editor of *Christianity and Crisis*, REINHOLD NIEBUHR is Vice-President of Union Theological Seminary in New York City. Though noted as a brilliant theologian and philosopher, Dr. Niebuhr is also a serious student of political affairs whose books and articles have influenced the thought of many outstanding leaders in politics and international affairs. "Religiosity and the Christian Faith," appeared in January, 1955.

EDITOR'S PREFACE

Though these articles were originally written for specific occasions and were not intended to appear together and though they may not appear on the surface to have a unity, there is a unity which underlies them all. This unity is seen in the fact that they have all been written from a perspective of Christian concern. This concern is expressed in a broadly social or cultural context, and it understands that exclusively individualistic piety is a perversion of the Christian faith. This unity is further notable in the fact that implicitly, if not explicitly, these essays, individually and collectively, represent the hope that there may be a transformation of at least some aspects of social, intellectual, or cultural life under the impact of the gospel.

There has necessarily been an element of subjectivity in the choosing of the essays which appear in this small volume. Some readers of *Christianity and Crisis* may feel a wiser selection would have been possible. Our major concern has been to gather a number of articles that would have a general appeal for Christian laymen and students who are concerned to think through the implications of faith for their life in the world about them.

The essays have been collected under the title, "What the Christian Hopes for in Society," and this is intended to point to a real coherence which is theirs. John Bennett deals directly with that subject as he attempts to set forth the tenable bases for a sober social hope, despite an awareness of the lack of any absolute securities in history and of the destructiveness of which men and nations are capable.

Francis Pickens Miller writes, out of his own experience, concerning the relationship of churches and individuals to the world of practical politics and presents an especially illuminating discussion of the meaning of faith for the activity of the Christian politician. The field of international politics is the background for Kenneth Thompson's treatment of the way in which Christian realism provides resources for understanding in the arena of political decisions, although there is no simple correspondence between religious truth and political necessities. The worth of programs of technical assistance to underdeveloped areas is discussed by Margaret Mead in an attempt to counter those misunderstandings which confuse a concern for the material needs of men with "materialism" and which fail to recognize the potential of technology as an instrument of spiritual creativity and Christian love.

In a somewhat different area, Amos Wilder illumines both the life of faith and the work of the artist as he discerns in the experience of artistic creativity an analogue of authentic religious experience. Paul Tillich elaborates the positive religious meaning of the tension between the certainties of the believer and the persistent questionings of the intellectual critic of religion.

The essays by Reinhold Niebuhr and David Roberts examine the perennial danger that the gospel will be subordinated to national pride and to elements of contemporary culture as substitute religions.

It is hoped that this book will contribute to a broadened understanding of the meaning of Christian faith in the context of the modern world.

The editor is grateful to Reinhold Niebuhr and John C. Bennett, Co-Chairmen of the Editorial Board of *Christianity and Crisis*, for their wise counsel, and he is particularly indebted to Arnold W. Hearn for his advice and assistance.

Wayne H. Cowan

WHAT THE CHRISTIAN HOPES FOR IN SOCIETY

John C. Bennett

WHAT CAN WE HOPE FOR IN SOCIETY?

Within the past half-century, men in the Western world have plunged from the highest expectations that they have ever held concerning their future in this world to the darkest fears that they have ever known concerning that future. This change has taken place in the minds and hearts of many of us. In this country the change has been more recent than in Europe. Even now the older expectation lives on in the minds of many of the older generation who have not been able to revise their earlier hopes with consistency.

This change of outlook in regard to the future has taken place within the churches as well as in the secular mind. Liberal Christianity shared the belief in progress that came to dominate the culture. It often gave New Testament sanction to this belief by identifying the kingdom of God with a new social order in history. It is only fair, however, to recognize that much liberal Christian thought preserved some checks on this expectation.

There are at least three forms of optimistic belief in progress which we should reject.

1. There was the tendency to make the expectation of progress the substance of religious faith in some Christian circles and to substitute it for Christian faith in a clear-cut manner outside the church. The idea of progress that had its source in the Enlightenment was deliberately conceived as an alternative to belief in divine providence and to Christian ideas of redemption. It became a self-sufficient faith. There can be no doubt that though this view of progress does depend upon the biblical assumption of the importance of human history, it is a complete distortion of the biblical outlook. It is opposed to Christianity and is the source of morally destructive illusions in its denial of a transcendent source of judgment upon history. One of the weaknesses of any such religion of progress is the sacrifice of most generations to those generations whose lot will fall near the fulfillment of history.

2. We must reject the idea that progress is inevitable. This was given its strongest support by the conception of biological evolution. It often involved the tendency to deal with human history as

though it were an aspect of nature. It left no clear place for human freedom. And yet I think that such criticisms are not always applicable. The idea of inevitable progress was often no more than the belief that the right must prevail. This was not a denial of human freedom but rather confidence that men would come to see and do the right.

3. The third type of expectation to be rejected is the assurance that the major sources of social evil can be removed in such a way that the gains we make in removing them are secure. This view does not involve the idea of inevitable progress in all respects and it avoids the excesses of utopianism. It is no more than the faith that the major obstacles to justice and freedom and peace among men can be overcome and that when they are overcome, there will be no danger of falling back into the darkness of earlier periods. I suspect that whatever conventional symbols of perfection in history may be used, most believers in progress would be glad to settle for this more sober expectation.

But it is precisely this sober type of assurance—along with all utopianisms—which has been taken away from our generation. As I reflect upon it, it seems clear to me that it is basically untenable and that our loss of it is not the consequence of some recent failure of nerve caused by Hitler or the atom bomb.

The classical Christian teaching about the universality and persistence of sin has not been the main *cause* of the rejection of this sober belief in progress though it is a *ground* for doing so. There are many shades of the historic doctrine, and its precise relationship to our problem was never fully developed in the New Testament because of a lack of interest in it. Not until men began to count on a future of indefinite length and not until they became aware of the degree of change possible in social institutions was the issue raised that we now face. When we consider some of the factors that make it difficult to believe in progress in this third sense, it becomes possible to see how they are related to Christian teaching about sin and especially to one element in that teaching: *the recognition that the deepest roots of sin are spiritual, that it is on the higher levels of human development that the most destructive perversions of human life appear.*

There are two contemporary experiences which very vividly bring home to us the truth in this Christian teaching, and these two experiences in themselves have done most to destroy in many of us the confidence in secure progress by which we had formerly been guided.

The first is the realization that at the very moment in which the technical means of developing world community are available and at the very moment when more people than ever are convinced that world community is essential if civilized life is to continue in the world, the division between two parts of the world has become so deep that we cannot now see any way in which it can be overcome. I do not say that it cannot be overcome, only that we cannot see the steps by which such a favorable change might come. The division is all the deeper because it is caused not only by differences of economic interest or by nationalistic rivalries, but by a spiritual chasm that for the present destroys communication between those on opposite sides of the conflict.

Other aspects of the situation illustrate the point that the most stubborn problems come at a high level of development. The very formation of larger and larger communities creates the possibility of more fateful forms of power. The world divided into two parts is in a more dangerous condition than if it were divided into many parts. Also, one result of man's scientific development has been the production of weapons of war which threaten the existence of every form of moral and social progress. To the increased size of the units of power and the increased destructiveness of the weapons of war we must add many techniques for controlling the minds of men which modern rulers possess. This situation which I have been describing results from perversions of reason and of idealism, from the misuse of some of man's most remarkable intellectual achievements.

My second contemporary illustration covers much of the same ground but it suggests to me even more poignantly the way in which the idealisms of men can become the instruments of terrible evil. There has been remarkable progress in the concern for social justice and, in many countries, in the social and economic institutions which give effect to this higher sense of justice. There are some quite remarkable advances in our own country in this respect for which we should be very thankful. And yet the just aspirations of the underprivileged and the generous idealisms of many of the privileged have been changed into the means by which the most efficient and most oppressive of all tyrannies has been imposed on many nations. This is the same development that divides the human race and threatens it with global atomic war. The totalitarian tyranny itself does not necessarily lead to anything better. It may be destroyed by revolution, but what will follow the revolution?

The point which emerges most clearly from these two illustrations is that the most destructive social evils of which we have knowledge appear on what, according to any previous conception of progress, have been high levels of intellectual and moral advance. It now seems all too clear that the various over-all solutions of the social problem which have been emphasized in the past two centuries by the believers in progress are not solutions after all. I refer especially to the belief that education, the development of the social sciences, the spread of democratic institutions, or the socialization of property would be the saving factor.

Each one of these factors is greatly to be desired. My point is that each one of them creates new problems and cannot by itself be regarded as a self-sufficient solution. Education, for example, is a great good, but it will always be difficult to get the right educators; and there is no way of insuring that the educational process will not be perverted by those who have the most political or economic power.

There are two other general considerations which support what has been said so far concerning the difficulty of believing in progress even in the third sense. The first is the fact that all solutions of social problems create unexpected new problems. The balance between such social values as freedom and order is very delicate, and it is natural that changes that seem good in themselves are made at the expense of one of these values in ways that are not fully understood in advance. An experimental shifting of emphasis from time to time in a reasonably stable society is to be expected and desired. But hazards become greater as the units of power become larger and the instruments of power more efficient. Such long-term trends as the development of technology, the increase of living standards, the growth of leisure, the elaboration of the mass media for entertainment and communication—all these create new and perplexing problems. But there is no turning back and it is our responsibility to do what is possible to redeem these instruments of "progress."

The second consideration is that spiritual advance from generation to generation is not dependably cumulative. Each generation has to learn its own lessons on the matters that are most important for its welfare. There is flexibility that is good in the fact that each generation rebels against its predecessor, but this very fact keeps moral gains from being secure. A strong spiritual impulse tends to lose momentum within a generation. If it is true, as I have suggested, that external gains are never secure gains, that institutional changes which promise much can be easily perverted if the spirit goes out of them, that in the precarious balance between freedom and order the responsible use of freedom and the self-disciplined exercise of power make all the difference—then this fact that we cannot count with assurance on the preservation from generation to generation of the loyalties and the sensitivities and the faith which are the chief sources of the health of a culture or of a social system is the factor which, more than any other, makes assurance concerning progress impossible.

So far I have been chiefly negative and have shown what we cannot believe about the future. Now as I turn to the things that we can believe, the result may seem less precise and, hence, anticlimactic. But my major interest in this article is to emphasize the elements of hope that remain.

There are no Christian guarantees of any particular good to be realized in the secular order, but there are Christian grounds for hope that man's cause in this world is no lost cause and that there will be significant embodiments of God's righteous purpose in human society. We cannot be sure of secure and cumulative progress in the moral quality of life or in the over-all welfare of the race. But every act of social justice, every corporate encouragement to the spiritual freedom of men, every achievement of true community is a gain even if we cannot promise that it will be followed by more and more of the same. The enormous technical advance creates possibilities of good that did not exist before. Take as an example the extraordinary extension of the life span, the improvement of health, the relief of suffering which are the results of the advance of medicine. All this is mostly gain though length of life may often lead to greater frustrations, and in the total picture the means of healing may be outweighed by the instruments of destruction.

History is not merely a platform on which individuals are prepared for inward blessings or for eternal life. Nor, as a record of man's collective life, is history a story of a vast and unified success. But within it there have been and there will be many communal and institutional embodiments of justice and fraternity which have value to the Lord of history. They are all of them partial and marked by man's sin as well as by true loyalty and love. If they pass away they remain as possibilities to be realized again. The record of them inspires generations that know them only as a memory. To work for such communal and institutional embodiments of justice and fraternity is to serve the kingdom of God, even though that kingdom far transcends them and by it all are judged.

The grounds for social hope which we find in Christian teaching are of two kinds—one related to God's creative work and the other to Christian redemption.

If we take seriously the idea that God is the creator and Lord of history, it is natural to infer from this that the structure of life is favorable to the continuation of his creative work. The belief that all men are made in God's image and the fact that Christians are encouraged to stress their own sin rather than the sin of other men, should undercut any tendency to cynicism about humanity in general. Calvin was surely right, as far as he went, in allowing for "common grace" in social life. In spite of a very dark view of the deformity of fallen man, he was able to write: ". . . as man is naturally a creature inclined to society, he has also by nature an instinctive propensity to cherish and preserve that society; and therefore we perceive in the minds of all men general impressions of civil probity and order"[1]* Augustine's insistence that there is no man

---

* All footnotes are found at the ends of chapters.

"so wholly abandoned to turpitude, but he hath some feeling of honesty left him" is similar. Augustine goes on to say that the devil must "change himself into an angel of light (as we read in the Scripture that he will do) if he is to effect fully his intention of deceit."[2]

A somewhat different phase of this basis for hope in God's creative work is the tendency of evil to be self-destructive. This has long been emphasized as a phase of the divine judgment in history. There is no comforting assurance that the process of judgment may not destroy most of the forces that make for good as well as those that make for evil, but there is strong pressure at work upon men today which causes them to see that they must find ways of living together more justly or perish. This kind of pressure by itself is not likely to bring men to a better society, but it has its positive value when combined with other motives.

We can see this process at work in international relations today. I have emphasized the tragic character of the East-West split in the world, but in spite of that we can say that the world has been brought closer than ever before to a recognition of the futility as well as the moral horror of war. There is fear in this and there is sheer fatigue in it. But there is also a widespread will to peace, the importance of which can be seen from the fact that the Communists can play on it so successfully. All this is important preparation for the development of the institutions of world community.

The interaction between these broad grounds for hope that we find in the creation itself and the redemptive forces that have been released as the result of the work of God in Christ is the heart of the matter. If we had only the redemptive forces to which to appeal, it is likely that we would think only in terms of a remnant to be saved out of the world. But it is the faith that the God of redemption is also the creator of the world which enables us to hope for more than that.

There is a quite remarkable converging of Christian thinking today, including New Testament studies, on the idea that the powers of the kingdom of God are already present within history. This emphasis upon the present kingdom is a more significant development in contemporary theology than the more widely publicized emphasis upon the hope for a future kingdom beyond history or a sophisticated conception of the "second coming." This idea of the present kingdom often takes the form of the rather difficult conception of the invasion of the future into the present, or the overlapping of present and future. We have to put the New Testament faith into a context that differs from the New Testament context at two points: the expectation of an indefinitely prolonged future and our better knowledge of the population of the whole world.

It seems to me that the strongest New Testament basis for hope for society is to be seen in the broad implications of this idea that the redemptive powers of the kingdom of God are present in history. The interaction of the redemptive powers of the kingdom with the factors that are favorable to social good in creation becomes relevant to our social hope when we see it in the context of an indefinitely prolonged future.

As I have warned so often, there is here no guarantee of any particular social good, but at least there is ground for hope that in ways beyond our present understanding the powers of the "age to come," the work of the living Christ, the influence of the Holy Spirit, the impact of that within the church which Paul Tillich calls the "New Being" will break through many of the obstacles in the secular order to transform and transform again the kingdoms of this world. Within human history we may not see the kingdom of this world become

the kingdom of God, but we may see among them
in many places and at many times communities,
institutions, and corporate acts of justice which
truly embody the grace and power of that kingdom.

To make this idea concrete I shall refer to a
recent event which had in itself some of the characteristics that such embodiments of the kingdom
must have. It is an event that took place outside the
sphere of what is usually regarded as Christendom.
It is an event that seems to me to symbolize most
of the real gains that have been made in recent
history. I refer to the recent Indian general election
in which a large proportion of the electorate voted
and which was remarkably free from corruption.
Let us grant that universal suffrage is no panacea,
that the new institutions of India are quite precarious, that the people may vote themselves into
totalitarianism. I accept all those reservations. But
does it not remain true that this event was a symbol
of the human dignity of all persons, of their participation in the common life, of their will to be free
from the control of another people? What had the
redemptive work of Christ to do with this event?
There was little direct influence from the church in
bringing it about, but it is unlikely that such an
election could have taken place without the indirect

influence of Christ upon Indian leadership and, we may add, without a Christian conscience in the country that yielded in time to Indian demands for independence. The acceptance of the importance of political action and the recognition of the essential equality of all human beings can be understood best against the background of such Christian influences. This event illustrates two aspects of every gain that is made in history. On the one hand, we know that it is insecure; on the other hand, we have good reason to thank God for it.

In conclusion, I shall bring together several considerations that need to be emphasized together.

1. The future should be regarded as open. There is no place for fatalism or for a dogmatic pessimism. Reinhold Niebuhr's phrase, "indeterminate possibilities," is a good way of indicating what we should think about the future. We must not face particular problems, no matter how difficult, with the idea that nothing constructive can be done about them.

2. We should not put any less emphasis than in the days of liberal optimism on the importance of large-scale events, of institutions, of the behavior of social groups. These are important because of what they do to persons.

3. We should avoid the tendency to allow many particular disappointments with the results of the great drive for social revolution, of which communism is but one expression, to cause us to swing to the conservative extreme. In particular, this means that we should distinguish between communism and the many efforts to bring about deep social changes which actually are an essential antidote to communism. Disappointment with the poor when they gain power should not tempt us to be less critical of the older forms of privilege. Disappointment with the results of social planning should not send us back into a one-sided emphasis on the freedom of the individual. We should have known long ago that the social revolution in any one of its many forms is no panacea, that it brings with it many new problems, but that these problems are on a level on which new and precious possibilities of justice for the vast majority of human beings are present for the first time in history.

4. The meaning of what we do does not depend only or even chiefly upon our correct calculations about future consequences. Our intentions must be directed toward the future and we have a responsibility to seek the best possible consequences. It is not enough to satisfy ourselves that our intentions

are good. Something more is necessary to save us from the anxiety which accompanies such decisions if we are to have Christian wholeness of spirit or even a troubled peace. This something more is faith that God will forgive us for the evil in our decisions and actions, that God will use them and us for the fulfillment of his purpose in ways beyond our calculation. The *motive* for action should not be hope, but love for all the people whose welfare is at stake in what we do or leave undone. The *direction* of action does depend upon some measure of hope, for if there were no hope of results we would in most cases change the course of our action. The *morale* for action depends upon faith. Hope is important but it is subordinate to faith and love.

FOOTNOTES

1. *Institutes*, Book II, Ch. ii, 13.
2. *The City of God*, Book II, Ch. 26.

Francis Pickens Miller

CHRISTIAN ETHICS
AND PRACTICAL POLITICS

It seems hardly necessary to define what we mean by Christian ethics, but I should like to make as clear as possible what I mean by Christian ethics. I do not, of course, mean a body of rules, principles, or precepts, or a system of teaching. By Christian ethics, I mean the moral insights and convictions which come to a Christian man in light of the Bible, through the historical experience and teaching of the Christian church, and out of his present fellowship in a community of believers as he faces the concrete situations of his own life.

Practical politics is somewhat easier to define. In America, it is the art of securing and maintaining the support of a majority of the voters.

The question is this: can Christian ethics be applied to practical politics? The answer is clear. Christian ethics can be applied to practical politics as well as to any other form of social action. In one sense, of course, Christian ethics can never be applied completely to any human activity, since no human activity can be perfectly ethical. Perhaps the use of the word "applied" is unfortunate. It might be better to rephrase the question to read: can Christian men engage in practical politics and remain Christian? The answer is that they can, and it is imperative that they should.

There are, of course, special difficulties for the Christian who enters the field of practical politics which are inherent in the nature of our American political system. For instance, the democratic politician has to appeal to a cross section of American society as it is. The cross section to which he makes his appeal for votes may and probably does include almost every conceivable American type. It will include believers and unbelievers, rich and poor, white and black, farmers, managers, and factory workers.

This situation leads inevitably to the question of compromise. In one sense, compromise is of the very essence of politics, if by that is meant compromising sufficiently the differences and interests that separate various groups in order to secure the support of all of them. It is also inevitable that the Christian who takes part in politics should find it necessary to advocate only a fraction of the program which he eventually hopes to realize. The question of timing and determining the maximum amount of change which is feasible at any given moment is extremely important for him. Proper timing is a very different thing, however, from compromise. Compromise occurs when a Christian either advocates aims which he knows are contrary to Christian ethics, or when he adopts a time schedule much slower than the conscience of the community justifies. His aim should be to maintain the maximum speed of change which will be tolerated by the community.

Another difficulty, which is closely connected with the other two, but which is, of course, no more peculiar to the American scene than to any other, is the question of means and ends. In order to attain ethical ends, is the Christian in politics justified in using means which are contrary to Christian ethics?

First of all, I believe that the Christian in politics should be as much concerned about his own ethical conduct as he would be in any other profession or vocation. I believe that Christian ethics are related to practical politics as much as they are to family life and that the same ethic applies to both. There is not one ethical standard for political activity and another standard for private life. I believe that ends never justify means and that if unethical means are employed to achieve ethical ends, the ends desired can never be realized in the Christian sense of realization. Further, my own experience is that a Christian is under no greater pressure to sacrifice his ethical convictions in practical politics than in any other form of human activity. I sometimes think that ecclesiastical politics is capable of exerting even more pressure for the sacrifice of ethical standards upon those who participate in it than is governmental politics.

The ethical dilemma which a Christian political candidate faces can best be illustrated by listing the types of choices he has to make:

1. He must choose carefully those aims he announces when he runs for office. Every aim, however trivial, should represent the expression of a genuine Christian concern.

The most important and, at the same time, the most perplexing policy aim with which a Christian in politics has to wrestle is the problem of governmental action on behalf of the general welfare—in other words, the problem of the function and limits of the welfare state. Where voluntary initiative is not feasible but, at the same time, action on behalf of the general welfare is necessary, Christians will favor such action being taken by the unit of government capable of performing the service required that is closest to the people concerned. In other words, if a job can be done by a county or town instead of by state or federal government, Christians in principle will prefer the local authority. The reason is that on the local level citizens can exercise their sense of responsibility much more directly and effectively upon the course of public affairs than they can when government is remote.

However, in this mass society which the machine has created, an increasing amount of governmental action will necessarily have to be taken on the state, on the federal, and even on the world level. It is obvious, for example, that in the United States of America a certain amount of federal government-guaranteed economic security is required to insure that citizens generally can enjoy responsible freedom.

The questions to which the Christian politician, therefore, must constantly be seeking answers are: (a) How can one measure the amount of government-guaranteed security required to insure that citizens generally enjoy responsible freedom? (b) How can one ascertain the point of optimum return from government action—the point at which the curves of responsible freedom and initiative cease rising and begin to decline if further security is guaranteed by government?

In a dynamic society, no fixed point can be established, and no permanent line drawn. But the main concern of the Christian statesman will be to define the point and draw the line as successive policy decisions have to be made. The maintenance of a proper balance between freedom and security is the essence of liberty as understood by the Christian conscience.

What the Christian in politics should not do is, as usual, clearer than what he should do. A Christian should never advocate an aim merely to secure a bloc of votes if this aim is contrary to the larger interests or to the general welfare of the state, the nation, and the world. He will never capitulate to the current assumption that it is necessary to outbid his opponent with economic or financial favors. And, however tempting it may be, he will never choose aims which appeal to the sub-Christian or subhuman in man, or which are calculated to arouse racial or class prejudice.

2. A Christian candidate also has to choose his lieutenants, and this choice is perhaps the most

difficult of all. He will have working for him men who are not Christians and men who don't have very much principle. When to maintain a friendship and when to break it for ethical reasons is the hardest decision the Christian in politics will have to make.

3. He will have to choose his campaign tactics. How hard will he hit? How personal will he become in his attack? Can he ever hope to win by keeping his campaign on a high impersonal level?

4. He will have to decide how to answer the tactics of his opponents. The Christian in politics can expect to be treated like a subversive character. He will be called every name that human ingenuity can invent, and he will be charged with every evil intention that seems at all plausible. How does he answer these attacks? When I have been faced with this problem, I must confess that the twenty-third chapter of Matthew has always been a great comfort to me. But better Christians than I disagree. Though he was the target of the most outrageous and villainous attacks ever launched against a candidate in the South, Frank Graham never attacked his opponent or replied to his tormentors. Was that the Christian way to fight a campaign?

5. He has to choose how his money is to be used,

if he has any. And even though he makes the right choices, he can never be sure that some lieutenant down the line may not use funds in a way that would horrify him if he were aware of it.

6. He has to decide how and on what grounds he is to appeal for the support of minority groups or racial groups. Is he to appeal to their race consciousness? Is he to profit by inflaming their sense of being wronged by the rest of the community? Or, is his appeal to be directed to lifting them up out of their self-consciousness and making them aware of their participation in and responsibility for the community as a whole?

Thus far, our experience in America with active Protestant Christians in politics has not been too encouraging. Unhappily, many Christians in politics tend toward one of two extremes. On the one hand, there is the kind of politically naïve Protestant who swallows the rottenest political bait hook, line, and sinker; and, on the other hand, there is the perfectionist to whom all public questions are either black or white, and who believes that the Christian must take his stand on absolutes which must be realized day after tomorrow. The perfectionist in his way discredits Christian ethics as much as the man who compromises his Christian ethics. What is wanted is an ethical sense of timing coupled with capacity to work with practical politicians without being taken in by them.

The Christian candidate or politician is not, however, the only one who has a responsibility in this matter. Christian citizens generally, as well as church leaders, have an equal responsibility for making clearer to the community as a whole the relationship between Christian ethics and practical politics. From the moment I first entered the political arena nearly twenty years ago, I have never ceased to be astonished by the absence of the capacity for righteous indignation among Christians as far as practical politics was concerned. Since the founding of the Republic, the assumption has been slowly built up that there are no ethical standards in politics and that "anything goes." No matter how revolting the incident, the normal comment of even a pious Christian is, "It's only politics!"

In August, 1951, an important primary election in the city of Richmond, Virginia, was won by the use of a diabolically clever, but fraudulent, letter. The letter was written as if from one Negro to another on a spurious letterhead entitled "Political Action Committee for Advancement of Colored People in America." The letter mentioned several candidates who should receive the support of Negroes, because they could be trusted to eliminate every form of segregation and secure for them their equal rights. The letter was not mailed to any Negroes, but went to several thousand white citizens. As a result, a Dixiecrat led the polls, and two candidates mentioned in the letter, whose defeat was desired by the authors of the letter, were driven from public life. In other words, a gigantic hoax and fraud had been perpetrated on the people of Richmond, but, so far as I know, not one church leader or church organization made any comment. Why is there no ethical leadership among Protestants in matters of this kind?

The effective functioning of government by consent depends upon (1) the basic liberties guaranteed by our Bill of Rights, (2) truthfulness, honesty, and integrity in the conduct of the public business, and (3) a sense of responsibility among the citizens generally for preserving their liberties and making their system of government work.

The conditions above are essential to the creation and survival of a free and responsible society. They are the product of Christian faith and life. If Christian faith and life disappear, conditions essential to a free and responsible society will also disappear.

The role of the Christian community in relation to public affairs includes (1) the proclamation of the Christian doctrines of creation, of redemption, of the nature of man and of the nature of human society as touchstones for political policy and action; (2) the continuous and fearless assertion of religious freedom; (3) the affirmation of ethical standards for public life and their application to specific instances; and (4) the sending of its ablest and most devoted young men and women into politics.

The responsibility of the church has to be considered in relation to various aspects of the church's life. These include (1) official church bodies, (2) ministers, and (3) laymen.

1. The official church body is responsible for public statements on grave ethical and spiritual matters of general concern. It should never attack or endorse a particular party or candidate unless religious freedom itself is in jeopardy or unless the body politic is in imminent danger of corruption from policies announced or methods employed. The failure of the Protestant Church in Europe to expose the evils of Nazism and fascism until it was too late is a warning which American Protestants cannot afford to ignore. An occasion may arise in

America when official church bodies should denounce a particular movement or trend in its incipient stages before the life of the nation as a whole has been corrupted.

One of the most disquieting aspects of American Protestantism at the moment is the silence of official church bodies on the most burning moral problems of our day. The phenomenon known as McCarthyism, character assassination as a method of achieving immediate political ends, the use of the Big Lie to win elections, and widespread venality in government—these are not merely symptoms of a decaying society: they are a denial of the mind and spirit of our Lord Jesus Christ. True Christians will do everything in their power to eradicate these cancers from the body politic and to expose those who are responsible for them.

Why then have the official bodies of the Protestant churches remained silent? Why have they said nothing and done nothing? The American cardinals of the Roman Catholic Church have spoken out in no uncertain terms, but the National Council of the Churches of Christ has not spoken. Are honest Protestant Christians going to have to look to the Catholic Church for moral leadership in matters of this kind? These questions must be answered if

American Protestantism is to continue to operate as a vital moral and spiritual force in the life of the nation.

2. The minister has one function to perform in the pulpit and another function to perform in his personal relations with members of the congregation and the community at large. As far as his sermons are concerned, what has been said above about official church bodies applies, except that in the case of the minister the application of ethical standards to specific cases is necessarily more personal and, hence, requires meticulous concern for fact and great charity, as well as capacity for white-hot righteous indignation. The most important function of the minister, however, is to encourage his laymen to assume their proper civic and political responsibilities as Christians. He can do this best through personal conversations, through the work of his men's club, and in many other informal ways.

3. The Christian layman is responsible for entering the political arena as a Christian and taking as active a part as his time and the circumstances will permit. Unless Christian laymen do this, our system of government will break down. It has not been working too well in recent years because we, as Christian citizens, have let politics go by default.

In conclusion, the question naturally arises, "Can a Christian who tries to conduct a political campaign according to the best Christian insights he has, ever expect to win?" The answer is that he may sometime, but the probability is that at the present stage of our national development he will lose more often than he will win. However, the fact remains that it is absolutely essential for Christians to engage in political activity, because merely by their campaigning they can influence the trend of political life and, also, witness to their faith. The current political scene is evidence of how few Christians ever hear God calling them to the vocation of politics. It isn't that God fails to call, but that we fail to hear, and because we fail to hear, the free world is in jeopardy. This constitutes a unique challenge to Protestant churches and to Protestant leadership.

Paul Tillich

RELIGION AND ITS INTELLECTUAL CRITICS

Criticism is by no means identical with intellectual criticism. There are many other forms of criticism. Religion, for example, is criticized not only by intellectual critics: it is also criticized by *religious* critics. For instance, it is criticized most harshly and radically by the prophets who turn against the traditional religious system which is maintained and preserved by priestly tradition and is distorted in the course of history. The prophet criticizes, but his is not intellectual criticism. It is through the ultimate power of the religion which he criticizes that he tries to separate the good from the evil in it. This was the case with the Reformers who criticized hierarchical distortions in the Roman Church on the basis of the ultimate principles, turning against the distorted forms which they found and, where they had to, separate the good from the bad, the true from the false, and the beautiful from the ugly.

What is *intellectual* criticism? Of first consideration is the nature of intellectual criticism of religion.
Intellectual criticism is argumentative. It gives reasons. It attacks the claim of religion to be true; the
claim that it has validity in an ultimate sense of
human nature and the human predicament; the assumption that it is necessary as an expression of the
human situation within the world. Intellectual criticism of religion attacks this claim, either completely
or in special manifestations of religion. Of course
this intellectual criticism can be combined with political, emotional, and religious motives, but things
which cannot be separated often must be distin-
guished.

What is the root of intellectual criticism? It is
man's intellectual power. *"Intellegere"* means literally "to read between," being able to read between
the facts and perceptions of our daily life. "Reading
between" is understanding these facts, what they
mean, how they are related, what their causes and
their effects are. "Intellectual" means "arguing" on
the basis of facts but transcending them. It means
knowing, taking in as knowledge, and sometimes as
certainty, something into the meaning of which we
have looked. This intellect which "reads between"
is always critical. It belongs to its very essence to be

critical. Intellect, if it follows its own nature, never accepts anything without asking a question about its nature and validity. This is something universally human. But intellectual critics are people who, in a special sense, question religion on the basis of intellectual reasons. They may be driven by emotional remembrances of their adolescence, by religious motives unaware of the distortion of religion, or by political ideas, but they use reasons. They are intellectual critics.

This leads me to the second consideration—characteristics of the intellectual and the conflicts with religion arising from these characteristics. The intellectual, as intellectual, questions everything which he encounters. He does not take anything whatsoever, at least not consciously and not intentionally, without asking a question about it. Let us not despise the human possibility to ask questions. Asking is one of the great expressions of human freedom. Asking means that we are not identical with the reality which we are and in which we stand and which surrounds us. We have it, but also do not have it. We ask for it. Asking always means some identity with and some separation from what we have. And if we want to understand what man is, there is perhaps no better door of entrance into his nature than an analysis of what "asking" means. It is one of the most ordinary and most profound appearances in all reality.

The intellectual is he who asks. The function which is universally human—to be able to ask questions—becomes in the intellectual a special function, the function which forms his character, the dominant function of his intellectual life. But if this is so, if asking becomes the dominant function of the intellectual, then a tension arises between the intellectual's radical will to ask and the immediate, blessed certainty of the religious man and woman in their religious experiences, traditions, and symbols. This conflict cannot be avoided. The intellectual also subordinates the religious reality to the function of asking—asking questions—and that means having distance and detachment from the religious reality. The religious man cannot admit this. The religious man subordinates everything else to his encounter with that which is his unconditional concern, his ultimate passion.

Still another characteristic of the intellectual is that in him the function of asking is necessarily skeptical. He doubts everything. There are two forms of the intellectual doubt. The one is a merely technical, methodological way of doubting, as the great philosopher Descartes described it when he started his meditations and founded modern philosophy in doing so. He doubted in order to establish a new system of rational insights: if possible, certainties; if not possible, at least high probabilities. But doubt can be something more serious than a methodological trick which every thinker and scientist must use. It can become an attitude—an attitude which makes any certainty impossible, which doubts even probabilities and thus loses the content of life and is driven into a feeling of emptiness which may or may not end in despair. In both cases there is an obvious conflict with the unquestioned certainties of an immediate unbroken religious belief. The skeptic is regarded as a danger, and he is even attacked on religious and moral grounds.

A third characteristic of the intellectual is his anti-authoritarian character. This has already been mentioned with regard to emotional terms, but now we come to it in terms of a rational attack on any possible authority. The intellectual does not deny factual authority, of course. If he is a scientist, he knows that he is dependent on the historian and *vice versa*. This kind of factual authority is present in every human being. But the intellectual does not accept authority in principle, namely, a place or a person in whom authority is invested. When religion says that its contents are based on revelation, then it has an authority which is authority in itself— authority in principle—authority which cannot be doubted, and so the intellectual rejects it.

A further characteristic of the intellectual is his discipline in the clarity and the consistency of his thinking, in the well-thought-out base of verification of every statement, in his infinite caution in making any statement whatsoever. And this, of course, produces a conflict with the ecstatic, unverifiable, daring anticipation of faith.

There is a last and negative characteristic of the intellectual: he often, or almost always, lacks sufficient criticism of the predominance of the intellectual function. Many intellectuals, perhaps most of them, many scientists, and many philosophers exercise a kind of naïve imperialism with respect to the intellectual function. They want to make this function all-controlling. And in spite of their radical, skeptical seriousness and discipline, they are naïve at this point. They have the naïve presupposition that reality as a whole is open in this way alone. If they are profoundly skeptical they say that reality in its deeper levels is completely shut off from man and cannot be reached by any kind of

thinking and that the intellectual should be satisfied
if he deals alone with the forms and structures of
thought and matters of science. Everything else he
should leave to the emotions. In doing so, he negates
any other key to reality and to our own being
except the key of intellectual asking. But if this is
so, then religion which claims to be a key to the
ultimate reality is no key at all, for it does not
approach reality with the intellectual function but
with another function which we call the experience
of the holy. Such a function is denied by the imperialism of the intellectual.

What are the concrete problems, the specific
points in the intellectual attack on religion? There
is a first group containing conflicts about factual
statements made both by science or philosophy and
religion. Such a conflict was the one which was
symbolic for our whole modern time between the
astronomy of Copernicus and Galileo and the statements of the traditional ideas and symbols of Bible
and church about the structure of the universe. Another was the fight about the biological development
of men which came into being through the Darwin-
istic movement and which produced the legal trials
when the church wanted to defend the nonbiological
origins even of man's bodily existence. Finally one

which is most actual today, the conflict concerning historical research of biblical literature—so-called "biblical criticism"—which deals with the Bible and its records as it would deal with any other book, namely, using the serious and honest historical criteria which every historian uses everywhere if he interprets documents of the past. This conflict is still going on and has not lost its sharpness after these two hundred years of struggle. This is one group of those who attack the intellectual on religion.

There is another group. It represents the attempt to explain religion by explaining it away, namely, explaining it away in nonreligious terms. It is the psychological and sociological explanation of religion represented by three names. One declares that religion is a projection of man's infinite desires for life and love into the heaven of the absolute. The man who did this was Feuerbach. Another who followed him and who did it in more complete psychological terms, saying that religion is based on the projection of the father-image into heaven, is Sigmund Freud. And the third, probably the most successful, said that religion is based on a projection of the social ideal into the earlier imagination of a transcendent heaven. This was Karl Marx. When I look at the history of Christian thought and defense, I think that these three attacks were and are the three most powerful ones. They have an extreme power of impressing themselves on the human mind. Much secularism, much negation of religion, is based on these three powerful, intellectual attacks and criticisms of religion.

There is a third more positive way. The intellectual establishes systems of thought which, with respect to religion, either transform it or deny it. The way in which religion is transformed by systems of intellectual thought is usually called idealism. Many a Christian as he hears the word "idealism" thinks, "Now we are saved; this man is an idealist." But they are not saved at all, as the history of Christian thought has shown. Idealism means taking religion as an element into a rational system of the world as a whole, and eliminating those elements of religion which we usually call the paradoxical character of the religious experience. And then the other system which is established by intellectual critics of religion is naturalism, which removes religious contents for the sake of a united world which has the characteristics of nature, whether in subhuman nature or in man. My judgment is that this second, more radical, attack is less dangerous than the former, less radical, and often very compromising attack.

Now I come to my fourth and last consideration,

namely, the justification of intellectual criticism and the possible answer of religion. The first and general justification of the attack of the intellectual is that man as man is an image of God only because he has the rational power to transcend the given, to criticize everything which he encounters, and he has this right also, as the image of God, to criticize that realm which deals directly with divine things—the realm of religion. Even more, he must accept this criticism as a religious necessity, and he never should use the arrogant attitude of calling this criticism, as such, human arrogance. This is the general justification of the intellectual criticism of religion, which must be accepted religiously in the name of man as free. Then, the second justification of the intellectual criticism against religion is the way in which religion competes with scientific work in factual statements about nature or about history. In the moment in which this is done religion demands the human intellect to become dishonest in order to accept religion. This is one of the most serious points. In the name of religion, religion must accept the autonomies, the freedom of scientific research in all realms according to the scientific methods which are the best ones in a special period, which may change, but which can change only through better insights of the scientific mind itself. Religion never should go down into the arena in which the sciences fight—be it in natural sciences, be it sociology, be it in psychology (which is very important today), or be it in history. Religion *qua* religion does not belong in this arena.

Third, religion has far too often been transformed into a system of statements which look like statements about the finite world of time and space. For instance, if somebody discusses the question, "Does God exist or does God not exist?" then he makes God into a being in space and time and asks a question as if he asked, "Does another galaxy exist or does it not exist?" God is blasphemed if his existence is discussed because he is beyond existence, as all classical theology knew. Here again, religion has to make it clear that it is not the same dimension in which religion experiences truth and in which people who deal with the world of the finite in time and space deal. Existence belongs to the world of time and space and not to the dimension of reality which we call the holy or the divine.

Another justification for intellectual criticism is the literalism which is still in the minds of some educated people as it justly is in the mind of primitive people now and in former centuries. People

who know the difference between the objective world
of time and space and the meaning of religion sin
against religion if they take its symbols literally
because then they provoke inescapably the asking
mind—the mind of the intellectual, its criticism, its
skepticism, and its radical wrath. What religion has
to do and is doing now, largely in the theological
world, is to rediscover that everything religious is
symbolic. Symbolic does not mean unreal. It means
more real than anything real in time and space.
Therefore, intellectual criticism cannot destroy it,
nor can intellectual defense protect it. This is also
true of biblical symbols which are absurd and
blasphemous if taken literally, but which are the
adequate expressions of truth if taken symbolically.

Religion should also accept one of the most
powerful criticisms of the intellectual, namely, that
the symbolic material is changing because the relationship to the ultimate is changing. Not the ultimate concern about God himself is changing, but
the concrete forms are changing. And when you
ask, "Is that valid also of the Christ?" then I would
say, "It is not, because the Christ in sacrificing his
temporal and special existence did not bind us to
any special forms of symbolism but transcended
them and became the spirit on which the church
is based."

Theology must accept the problem of verification. Why is something which religion says true? The intellectual says, "We need detached observation." Religion answers, "You need that; we need it in some respects; but we need first of all, something else, namely participation and risk." Religion is always risk, and verification in religion is never the verification of physical experiment, but it is always the verification of a life risk. Somebody says, "I surrendered; I devoted my life; I accepted this; and I took a chance. It was not, by any means, scientifically verified, but perhaps the risk failed." Or, "The risk was right," but it is impossible to know this beforehand. Now this is the verification of religion—spirit and power as it is called in the New Testament. This is the pragmatic element of risk which we need against any dogmatic absolutism.

Now let me close with one idea which came to me while I was thinking about these problems. The most important thing religion can do about the intellectual critic is to take him into the religion itself, to take him into the totality of the religious life. That was done by the early church and has been done ever since in the churches. And the name of this man who is an intellectual and is taken into the totality of the religious experience is "theologian." And from this follows the meaning and the significance of the theologian. The theologian is both. He is the intellectual critic, and he is the representative of what he criticizes. The theologian is he who represents in himself the whole conflict, the whole weight and difficulty of the conflict which I have been describing. This is his misery and perhaps sometimes his glory.

There are different ways in which different religions accept this situation. In the Roman Church the theologian has been, in the course of the two thousand years of the development of this church, more and more subjected to the tradition and the authority of the church. He has, as a Roman Catholic theologian, lost the possibility of radical questioning, of asking in a radical and uncompromising sense. The Protestant has rediscovered the theologian as somebody who, although he stands within the whole of religion, is able to accept the criticism which he has in himself in all the different forms which I have described. And it is the greatness and the weakness of Protestantism that it is able to have the intellectual critic of religion in its own midst, but perhaps, in the long run, this is the only way in which the relationship of these two human possibilities can be ordered. Our country is in a situation in which the intellectuals are, generally speaking, under attack.

Many church people are happy about this removal of the intellectuals from public influence and from the permission to ask the radical questions. But do not be happy about this in the name of religion. It is a fascist form, to use this general word, which *always,* and I can speak out of experience from Nazism, first turns against the intellectuals because radical questions should be excluded. But even more important than this political danger is the spiritual danger of the fight against the intellectual critic, namely, the danger that religion become superstition. Every religion which cannot stand ultimately the radical question that is asked by the intellectual critic of religion, is superstition.

David E. Roberts

THE CHRISTIAN GOSPEL AND
THE AMERICAN WAY OF LIFE

When I was in Germany in the early 1930's I became acquainted with a New Testament scholar who
was at the same time a Nazi. As a student fresh from
the halls of Union Seminary, I was completely
baffled by the mentality of this man. His knowledge
of the New Testament was not only technically com-
petent; it was accompanied by religious passion and
theological sincerity. Yet I could not fathom how
anyone could be so intensely devoted to the gospel
and be a Nazi at the same time.

In my memory he stands as a vivid illustration
of the fact that what a man allows the Bible to say
to him is profoundly influenced by the situation in
which he finds himself. A powerful ideology had
taken control of the consciousness of Germany. This
man was cut off from other ideas. He could have
lost his job and been thrown into a concentration
camp for defending an unpopular point of view.

Therefore, something more compelling than his own scholarship easily dictated what he was able to think and say. Circumstances had arisen where it was almost impossible for him to allow himself to grasp the real import of the New Testament, because that would have been too dangerous.

Surely the predicament of this German scholar illustrates a principle which goes far beyond his own situation. In a sense, it is always too dangerous for men to grasp the real import of the New Testament —any time, anywhere, in any society. This is because the gospel always lays bare elements of tyranny which society regards as necessary for its own security. It lays bare the hollowness of every quest for earthly power, prosperity, and triumph. It gives the lie to our feverish boast that we are "only trying to defend justice." It debunks every human virtue which falls short of the humility of love. In a stubborn, inconvenient way, the New Testament holds out against all ordinary definitions of power, success, and righteousness.

Therefore, it is a dangerous thing for anyone to try to look at *American* life in the light of the gospel. To be sure, men do not get thrown into jail here very often just for preaching. But in cynical moments one might suspect that this is partly due to the fact that we preachers have failed to make clear the real nature of the book we have on our hands. The New Testament is a highly subversive document. If it is taken seriously, it prevents people from giving unqualified devotion to current definitions of the American way of life. And precisely because the pulpit is still so free, even a comparatively timid preacher is without excuse if he tries to conceal this fact.

We can best manifest our loyalty to American traditions of religious and political liberty by exercising the God-given right of looking at ourselves in the light of his Word. Let us pass over, as too familiar, the reflections which come to mind when we tally up the newspaper accounts: dope-addiction among adolescents, bribery of college athletes, the power of organized crime, the corruption of government officials. I agree with those who declare that the only long-range remedy for such moral disintegration is a return to faith in God. But I get weary of hearing the declaration repeated because there is so little likelihood of increasing our national understanding of the gospel by representing it as a sort of emergency supplement to the police force.

Certainly the extent of our moral disintegration is connected with a religious disintegration. But we cannot even come in sight of a radical religious recovery until the churches and the people of this country begin to do penance for the way we have tried to pour the new wine of the gospel into some peculiarly American bottles.

Many of the proposed alliances between Christian ideals and American ideals that we hear about today are actually a threat to both, for they fit perfectly into the pattern of all fanaticism. The fanatic knows, at some level, that he is living a lie. And because his case cannot bear scrutiny in open debate, he is compelled to ward off the threat of exposure by means of catch-phrases, righteous indignation, and sanctions. Indeed, within one set of premises many of our home-grown fanatics are virtually irrefutable, and they possess specialized forms of information and power which can make their total case seem plausible. If you grant that the greatness of our nation is to be judged primarily in terms of its standard of living, its efficiency, its military power, then everything else follows. So long as moral and religious considerations are left out, their case is consistent and impregnable. Strangely enough, however, most Amercans are not crass enough to leave out such considerations—at least when they are speaking in public. That is where the inconsistency enters in; and that is where the defensive rationalization has to begin. The advocates of a case which makes sense in terms of pure power-politics want at the same time to claim that they are following faith in God and preserving the ethical foundations of democracy.

A recent letter in *The New York Times* reads, in part, as follows:

"Our nation was founded and brought to greatness by men who had an unquestioning faith in God. . . . [But] signs of a collapse of conscience in these United States are to be found everywhere. . . . If we are to survive as a great nation we must turn again toward the ideals and the simple faith that made us great. We must reaffirm our faith in the dignity of man and in the rightness of our democratic way of life under God."

So far, so good. But then the writer continues: "I do not propose to offer a solution to the vast problem . . . now confronting . . . our country. But I do suggest that a start in the right direction might be made in our schools and colleges. . . . Today . . . an entirely false concept of academic freedom is turning our colleges into booby traps for young and impressionable minds. Evil and alien influences are brought to bear upon youths who lack the maturity and understanding to discriminate between philosophies, and to winnow the good from the bad. . . . Too often today the American way of life—from a belief in free enterprise to faith in democracy—is belittled by our . . . professors. The time has come to have done with such corroding nonsense."

Precisely because this letter is by no means fanatical in tone, it well illustrates the conjunction of ideas which is so widespread—and so dangerous. The author begins by talking about faith in God, the dignity of man, and the rightness of our democratic way of life. But he ends by attacking those methods whereby *alone* young men can learn to discriminate between good and evil philosophies. Undoubtedly he is not aware of any inconsistency. Yet how can faith in the dignity of man be expressed by choking the growth of critical intelligence and independent judgment? How can confidence in the superiority of free enterprise be expressed by shutting off open debate? Above all, how can religious faith be restored by associating it with national pride instead of with Christian penitence and forgiveness? The letter as a whole makes one feel that the author is a sincere man of high principles. That is part of the tragedy of our country and our churches today. So many fine people have fallen unconsciously into forms of religious confusion and moral duplicity which are just as bad as those they are trying to fight.

Nevertheless the fact remains that there can be no return to faith in God so long as he is regarded as a sort of confirmatory appendage to the American way of life. Actually we are confronted with a clear-cut choice. *Either* the New Testament is to be supreme, and we are to judge our nation in the light of its standards of righteousness and spiritual greatness, *or* the so-called American way of life is to be our substitute religion, and the church is to be its mouthpiece. In the latter case, our situation is not unlike that of the Nazi professor, where men hear only those portions of the gospel which seemingly confirm their national aims and assumptions.

The mentality we have been examining, then, is not really an ally of Christian ideals. Neither is it an ally of the democratic way of life. Those who proclaim their allegiance most loudly are seldom to be found in the forefront of movements which implement democratic principles in racial and economic relations. On the contrary, they regard such movements as dangerously liberal, and then they lump liberalism with communism.

In the recent book, *Civil Liberties Under Attack*,

one of the authors mentions the case of a government official with an impeccable record who was placed under charges because unidentified informers asserted he "advocated the Communist Party line, such as favoring peace and civil liberties," and "his convictions concerning equal rights for all races and classes extend slightly beyond the normal feelings of the average individual."[1]

Now why do we find this widespread panic, this unconscious dread of genuine democracy, among those who claim to be its guardians? There is no single nor simple explanation. Perhaps our actual situation in the world is precarious enough to drive some people—especially those with extensive possessions to lose—into a defensive form of hysteria and a search for scapegoats. But why the need for scapegoats? Part of the answer is that many of our one-hundred-per-cent-American patterns of life are flatly incompatible with democracy, and we don't want to admit it.

Democracy stands or falls on the attitude toward the person. The question is not merely whether he is free, in a technical sense, to vote, to work, to speak and to worship. The question is also whether he is looked upon as a responsible, spiritual being instead of a cog in a social machine. Who could read the

recent article in *Life* magazine about corporation
wives without seeing in it an example of how the
genuinely personal gets stifled? Here the suitability
of a man's home life, his wife and his children must
be judged in terms of how efficiently they function
in tooling him up for another day's work. The wife
is to engage in "reading and music and that kind of
stuff" so that she will seem cultured when she meets
her husband's associates. The suburb they choose to
live in, the size of their car, and their circle of
friends must properly reflect his status; and they
must change, with exquisite timing, as he moves up
the ladder. The article goes on to say that "roughly
half of the companies on which *Fortune* has data,
have made wife-screening a regular practice and
many others seem about ready to do so. . . . 'Suc-
cesses here,' says one official, 'are guys who eat and
sleep the company. If a man's first interest is his
wife and family, more power to him—but we don't
want him.' 'We've got quite an equity in the man,'
another explains, 'and it's only prudence to protect
it by bringing the wife into the picture.' "[2]

Surely we miss the point if we simply rant against
the corporation. The corporation is, willy-nilly, part
of a wider pattern. And the wider pattern is nothing
less than a creeping, totalitarian religion. It is a

religion because it dictates how a person shall find security, self-esteem, standards of value, and reasons for living. It is totalitarian because, although one has some mobility within the pattern, one has lost the basic freedom of departing from the pattern itself. All of us are caught in it to some extent; that is why so many of us have to disguise its real character by talking about individualism, free enterprise, and democracy; and that is why so many of us have to go looking for scapegoats. We don't dare look at how standardized, collectivized, and conformist we are. If we can find a scapegoat, we are spared having to face ourselves.

Yet this substitute religion—which is *the* most potent factor in the lives of many Americans—is not only irreconcilable with Christianity, it is not even a worthy form of humanism. It undercuts all the valid reasons for "reading and music and that sort of stuff." It destroys the basis for real friendship by making uncalculating appreciation of others almost impossible. It forces men who are presumably capable of having respect and affection for their wives and children as persons, to view their loved ones as economic functions.

Significantly enough, the article in *Life* says nothing whatever about the young executive, or the young wife, who might have convictions which run counter to prevailing views on economic and political questions. And I am quite ready to believe that *they no longer exist.* Yet what has happened to the bold iconoclasm on which the democracy of this country was founded? What has happened to the independent thinking of the individual? In business, in the entertainment field, in journalism, young men will tell you that their exercise of independent judgment and their advocacy of "democracy" must fall within prescribed channels, it must be associated with "safe" political and economic doctrine—or else. Or else they might just as well look for some other sort of work. The same thing is becoming increasingly true in our colleges. Are the churches next on the list?

In the light of all this, we should be profoundly afraid for the welfare of our country. But we should be more angry than afraid, and more resolved than angry. It is not too late to win the battle against a creeping, totalitarian religion which has arisen within the most respectable centers of our national life. We must wage the struggle as strenuously as we fight against communism and all other external threats to liberty, and for precisely the same reason. What is at stake is not simply the welfare of America, but the hope of the human spirit throughout the world. Thank God, there are still plenty of people who really believe that the integrity of personality comes first in a definition of democracy and that the rightness of our economic and political policies must be judged by this standard.

But if the strength of this ethical conviction is to be restored, it must be based upon a recovery of the core of our religious heritage. That means we must disentangle the Christian gospel from every attempt to ally it with economic selfishness or national pride. The church can play its part in keeping alive freedom of speech, freedom of conscience, and freedom of worship only if it uses them to the hilt. It must care more about truth than about expediency, and it must fear God instead of men. Are we not embarrassed, as Christians, that the armed forces have moved faster than the churches toward solving the problem of racial segregation? We are truly ludicrous when we run behind secular agencies, instead of ahead of them, in the struggle for democracy. If we love our country, if we care deeply about its potentialities for true greatness and service, we must oppose at the political level and by political means those who are ruining it while they stridently claim to be defending it. And at the religious level, if we love the church, we must oppose every movement which tries to interfuse its teachings with hatred, self-righteousness, and reaction. Everything precious in Protestantism is threatened wherever liberty itself is threatened. We are thoroughly aware of the enemies outside the gates. But if we are slain, it is just as likely to be by enemies within, who profess allegiance not to Stalin or the Pope, but to "Christian, i.e., American-way-of-life, freedom."

Surely the words of Lincoln are applicable to our situation: "The dogmas of the quiet past are inadequate to the stormy present. The occasion is piled high with difficulty, and we must rise with the occasion. As our case is new, so we must think anew and act anew. . . . [For] we shall nobly save or meanly lose, the last, best hope of earth."[3]

FOOTNOTES

1. *Saturday Review of Literature*, Jan. 12, 1952, p. 8.
2. *Life*, Jan. 7, 1952, pp. 32 ff.
3. Abraham Lincoln, Annual Message of Dec., 1862.

Margaret Mead

CHRISTIAN FAITH
AND TECHNICAL ASSISTANCE

The revolution that has taken place in the last decade in our capacity to speed up technological change has confronted the Christian churches with an ethical dilemma of no small proportions. Throughout the last two thousand years, Christianity and Judaism have provided the religious ethic which gave meaning and purpose to the attempts to ease the misery and lighten the darkness of the slave, the serf, the peasant, the heathen, and the aboriginal inhabitants of the newly discovered continents and islands beyond the sea.

In the Judaic ethic, to heal, to teach, and to feed the poor were good deeds, benefiting the giver, in fact benefiting the giver to such a degree that the recipient was hardly expected to reciprocate with more than formal deference. Similarly, in traditional Christianity the care of the sick, teaching the ignorant, and feeding the hungry were all works

through which individuals, acting in Christian compassion and charity, walked more closely in the
ways of the Lord.

This position was congruent with the state of
technology during the first nineteen hundred years
of the Christian Era. Christian compassion for suffering loomed far larger than Christian ability to
cure disease; Christian charity might succor and
help the needy, but the Great Famines and the Black
Death raged across Europe; Christian piety and
devotion might reproduce manuscripts by hand, but
universal literacy waited upon printing, mass production of books, and the audio-visual methods of
the twentieth century. From the kitchens of monas-
teries and colleges there might be distributions to
the poor at Christmas of lumps of meat the "size of
a child's head," and within convents the children,
left after plague and famine swept the land, might
be lovingly reared. Against plague, famine, and ignorance, these were slender bulwarks indeed. Religion counseled resignation to the will of God, and
tempered the bitterness and rebellion of those whose
children died one by one in infancy, or remained
the sole survivors of some plague. As compassion
was the appropriate active Christian virtue for
those who ministered to the unfortunate, so resig-

nation was the equally appropriate virtue in those who must bow their heads before a series of misfortunes which we would today account as preventable.

Meanwhile, both compassionate service and gentle resignation were reinforced by an other-worldliness which despised material things, even while distributing bread to the starving, or bathing the terrible sores on the feet of those who had no shoes in winter. This other-worldliness could survive even while using as good symbols those tools by which men gained their bread and journeyed over the seas to obtain new foods—the plough, the sickle, the ship— these were symbols which could be combined with the deepest religious devotion. Then came the machine, the substitution of fuel for men and women walking treadmills, the substitution of mechanical processes for the weariness of human hands. At first the machine seemed to be enslaving the human spirit rather than releasing it. As men and women entered the mines and factories, it seemed clear that the machine was Moloch devouring the souls and bodies of newly urbanized, lost, exploited human beings. The plough, the sickle, and the sail remained symbols of simple Christian goodness, of the yielding earth, of the good grain reaped in the fields, and of the traveler for whom one prayed, but the machine which was to increase the yield of the land and make the journeying traveler safe became identified with Mammon. The machine and all its works were evil—set against the vision of a New Jerusalem that might instead be built in England's green and pleasant lands. As the products of the machine grew, men came to live in cities which became more identified with godlessness. Materialism, industrialism, and urbanism became a trilogy of the works of the devil—an emphasis which was not lessened by the emphasis of Bolshevik propaganda upon godlessness coupled with the new deification of the machine.

So today we find ourselves in a parlous state. Since World War II the new technology, combined with the upsurge of aspiration and hope among all the peoples of the world, means that we confront a possibility of preventing hunger and premature death and of opening up the opportunities of literacy and experience beyond the wildest dreams of only a few decades ago. We confront this prospect not with the full vigor of religious dedication, but with divided hearts and minds, with a doubt whether anything born of the machine can be good, with a fear that it is materialistic to plan, to import tractors, or to set up assembly lines, to wear mass produced goods, buy paper books, or even—for some recently Christianized primitive peoples—to want shoes. A religious ethic attuned to compassion and resignation in a world of suffering and poverty is confused and stumbling in the face of a possible world where no one need go hungry, or die for want of a known remedy, or go ignorant and illiterate through life.

Communism and its adherents experience no such confusions. However much their methods may compromise their ends so that they are unattainable, they are clear in the congruence between health, education, and welfare, on the one hand, and the Communist ethic on the other, and young Soviet delegates to international congresses are moved to genuine tears by stories of land reclamation in some valley of starving peasants. The full vigor of their belief that food, health, and education are the most worthwhile ideals to pursue, for themselves and for other men, can go out to meet the awakened hopes of the hungry, ignorant, disease-ridden peoples of the jungles and deserts of the undeveloped countries of the earth. Meanwhile, the minds of Christian missionaries abroad and Christian people at home are divided; in their insistence that men do not live by bread alone, they are unwilling to let their hearts be kindled by the possibility that all men may have bread. All too often the enthusiasts who are dedicating themselves to the cause of technical assistance, fighting for more appropriations, seeking to develop ways and means of harnessing the skills of part of the modern world to the service of the rest of the world, must work with only their own secular zeal to sustain them, without benefit or backing from the churches. "The mission told us the Truth, but they did not show us the way," say the awakening peoples of the Pacific Islands, rebelling against teaching which told them "the Truth about the beginning of the world," but did not "tell us how to keep our babies from dying or our people from dying as young men."

The failure of the Christian churches to pick up this unprecedented hope for the peoples of the earth and to carry it as a sacred trust as part of their task of cherishing and protecting "the lives of men and the life of the world," is paralleled by another ethical dilemma—the desire to exploit technical assistance, to make feeding and teaching and curing people into a bribe, to keep the peoples of other countries on our side against communism. Over and over again, one hears the argument that technical assistance is good policy, the only way to hold back the march of communism. This is an appropriate argument in the mouths of those who believe that other men will do good deeds only for their own ends and is of a piece with setting up school lunch programs, not to feed children but to dispose of surplus agricultural products. Surely, holding back the tide of communism—or, put in religious terms, fighting the Devil—is a lesser good than cherishing God's children. How can we pause in a discussion of how, if we will, we can bring relief from hunger and pain and ignorance to millions, to suggest that it is also sound national policy? The invocation of this lesser good somehow dims and detracts from the shining purpose with which the vision of what can be done today should be able to infuse the imagination of contemporary Christians. Christ said, "Feed my lambs," and today there is the possibility of food enough to feed all his lambs; he said, "Heal the sick," and with aureomycin and sulfa, malarial control, immunization and vaccines, "they can be healed." Instead of this vision of a Christian ethic of the brotherhood of man which is realizable here on earth now, we have "technical assistance as a useful adjunct of national policy," suitably combined in small proportions with bilateral agreements involving the instruments of warfare. This produces an ethical misalliance between defensive warfare—which can never be defined by religious people as anything but an evil which may nevertheless be absolutely necessary if the conditions which are necessary for religion are not to disappear from the earth—and sharing life and hope between the technically advanced and the technically unadvanced peoples of the world. When technical assistance is thus reduced, either to an instrument of anticommunism or to an instrument of purely national policy, it no longer can completely command the religious imaginations of men.

In discussions of Point Four, it is customary and relevant to point out that many of the issues involved are already familiar to Americans who have given willingly of their substance and their lives to bring the gospel and to bring medicine and education and food to the peoples of other countries. However, they have not done this as Americans, but as American Christians, as particular groups of Christians, Methodists, or members of the Society of Friends, Episcopalians, or Baptists. Even in secular activities of sending food and clothing abroad, Americans have traditionally been extremely generous as individuals or as members of voluntary organizations, but grudging and stipulating when it came to Congressional action for the same ends.

European observers have often been confused by the apparent paradox of Americans who, in response to an appeal for voluntary abstention from essential foods, responded so magnificently in World War I and who in World War II expressed continuous anxiety for fear we would "starve to death" if we tried to feed the world. Yet the difference is quite explicable. I remember discussing this with a high official abroad during the war who said, "Anyway, you Americans are not going to export the food that is needed. You are going to eat it up yourselves." When I objected vigorously that the American people had shown over and over again their generosity, their willingness to give up butter and sugar that others might not starve, that because in this war it was government planned, people had not understood the need, he said, "Go home, and find a religious leader who will be willing to make the people understand." But there was no such religious leader ready; the groups who tried to make Americans realize that a decision not to ration soap would be translated into nutritional deprivation for millions of children were led by left-wing groups with suspect motivations. The actual enormous contribution—which should still have been much greater—that the United States Government made to feeding the world was virtually without benefit of clergy and loomed in the minds of the American people, not as too little—which they would have considered it had they acted privately and voluntarily, as Christians rather than as federal tax payers—but as too much.

Our ambivalence, as Americans, about the role of the federal government, at home and abroad, is a compound of our dislike of the federal government's getting into habits of playing Santa Claus and our dislike of anyone receiving hand-outs. The genius of the Point Four program was that it emphasized the role of Americans, acting through the federal government, in providing "know-how" rather than goods, in helping other peoples to help themselves. As such, there is much in the Point Four program which can catch the imagination and enlist the devotion of Americans—as Americans, and as Christians. If there were no other way in which technical assistance could be brought to Iran or Indonesia, then Point Four would represent one of our highest possible aspirations, perhaps exceeding, in dramatic if not in real value, the activities of voluntary associations of Americans, because the United States Point Four program has to operate in a world where national states take on either the true aspects of the bellwether of the flock, or that of wolves in sheep's clothing.

But Point Four operations are not our best invention because we have already conceived and designed an even better way, a way that is more compatible with the practice of the brotherhood of man. In giving technical assistance today and helping other peoples to overcome starvation, ignorance, and preventable disease, we have the choice of acting bilaterally, as members of a single, very rich, very prosperous, generous, but necessarily self-interested (for it is the function of national governments to protect their own people against all others) nation-state, or as members of an associated group of nations, in which we who wish to help and they who need help meet in an equality of interest and dignity. If Christian generosity and Christian giving are to be congruent with those democratic institutions which visions of the brotherhood of man under the fatherhood of God have done so much to foster, then any discrepancy between giver and receiver which can be wiped out must be wiped out. Simple sharing, not lordly benefaction, ennobles both giver and receiver while the least extra, unnecessary, in a sense technological discrepancy, begrimes and demeans such sharing.

Within the framework of the United Nations Technical Assistance program, all the members— the United States, Venezuela, France, Indonesia, Norway, although some are larger and stronger, some highly developed technically, some beginners in the task of putting modern science at the service of their peoples—act on a basis of equality within an organization which is their own. When the government of Venezuela or Greece asks help from the United Nations Technical Assistance program, it is one member of a group of brothers asking help from their own group, not the poor asking the rich, or the weak the strong, or the unskilled the technically trained. The United Nations may have to recruit all the technicians from the highly developed countries, but within international teams these men will work—in dignified, guaranteed equal status— with the representatives of the countries who have asked for assistance. As the richest country, the United States may foot the largest bill, not as a single benefactor of the mendicant peoples but as one among the peoples of the world.

Point Four, if stated as a way in which we, the fortunate, may help those less fortunate, has high ethical appeal in focusing the moral energy of Americans, as citizens, on the responsibility of the United

States in the modern world. But, as Kipling emphasized long ago in his much misunderstood poem, "The White Man's Burden," the task of the more technically developed country—the country whose technology, or religion, or political institutions bear the marks of generations of high-level concerted felicitous effort—is to make the recipients of help not into sycophants or dependents but into peers. Within the framework of the United Nations, all member peoples are peers, and it is the stated aim that the peoples of Trust Territories be helped to become full self-governing peoples also. Here there need be no confusion between Christian sharing and more limited national interest, no puffed-up pride of superior nation status. The people of any nation who proclaim themselves Christian have a role in regard to other nations in which no incompatible or partial aim need confuse the full involvement of their religious dedication.

But—even granted the partial suitability of Point Four, the more complete suitability of United Nations Technical Assistance progress as the structural expression of the brotherhood of man under the fatherhood of God, where no brother should set himself up above another—we are still in difficulty. We still have with us Christian ambivalence about the fruits of the machine, Christians' willingness to brand (as I have heard it branded by men in holy orders) the desire of mothers that their babies should not die as "materialism," Christians' willingness to denounce the machine—which as the successor of plough, sickle, and mortar, has made it possible for men to live more worthily of their humanity—as the enemy of spirituality. Under an elaborate superstructure which sometimes also draws help from the specious argument that people's cultures should be respected (an argument which got short enough shrift when it was a matter of giving other people the full details of our culture-laden religious ideas) too many Christians have drawn aside their skirts from the "materialism" of a program that will teach the hungry how to feed themselves. They thereby continue to support the Christian virtues of compassion and resignation, which were appropriate to the *inevitable* sufferings of man. But they do so in the context of the midtwentieth century, in which hunger and ignorance and epidemic disease are no longer inevitable, but definitely, immediately preventable.

The religiously gifted know, centuries early, what men pray for for other men, and in conclusion I should like to quote from an old Elizabethan prayer:

They that are snared and entangled in the utter lack of things needful for the body cannot set their minds upon Thee as they ought to do; but when they are deprived of the things which they so greatly desire, their hearts are cast down and quail for grief. Have pity upon them, therefore, most merciful Father, and relieve their misery through Thy incredible riches, that, removing their urgent necessity, they may rise up to Thee in mind.

Thou, O Lord, providest enough for all men with Thy most bountiful hand. . . . Give meat to the hungry and drink to the thirsty; comfort the sorrowful, cheer the dismayed and strengthen the weak; deliver the oppressed and give hope and courage to them that are out of heart.

Have mercy, O Lord, upon all forestallers, and upon all them that seek undue profits or unlawful gains. Turn Thou the hearts of them that live by cunning rather than by labour. Teach us that we stand daily and wholly in need of one another. And give us grace, in hand and mind, to add our proper share to the common stock; through Jesus Christ our Lord.

Amos N. Wilder

ARTIST AND BELIEVER

The life of the artist offers many analogies to the life of faith. The strictness of his way of life, the combination of *ascesis* and joy, the law of incarnation which limits all false spirituality: such features of the artist's calling carry both rebuke and instruction for the Christian, especially in a time when indulgence and unreality have infected the practice of religion. In today's cultural disarray, moreover, the modern artist in particular has much to teach us bearing on the rediscovery of meaning, the sifting of traditions, the discernment of spirits, and the renewal of the word. The problem of communication for the church today is no less urgent than for the artist. Our elaboration of a new grammar and rhetoric of faith and apologetic can learn much from the new discourse of the poets.

Consider the following passage from Rilke's *Les Cahiers de Malte Laurids Brigge*,[1] which may be taken as a parable of the religious life and of the fruit it may bear, of how greatness comes to birth.

The young Brigge has written some poetry. Yet, he comments, how little poetry amounts to when written in youth. After a long life, yes, at its very end, after all the buffeting and the myriad and cumulative situations and confrontations—then perhaps one could write ten lines of good verse. For poetry is not constituted by sentiments (those, indeed, come early enough) but by life experiences.

> To write a single line one must have seen many cities, men and things. . . . One must have had the memory of the groans of child-birth, and of the pale and sleeping forms of those who have given birth, their bodies now disburdened. One must also have been with the dying, have watched by the dead with the window open to the sounds of the world's stir outside. And it is not enough to have memories. . . . It is only when within us they have become blood, outlook, gesture, when they no longer have any name and are indistinguishable from ourselves, it is only then in some rare unexpected moment, out of all this, that the first word of a poem may arise.

This testimony of a great poet offers its clues for the believer, for neither is religion constituted of sentiments. Life is full of sentiments—lavish, potent, and exquisite—but they are not the important thing. Many no doubt confuse them with true spirituality.

Indeed, because they are rebuffed in seeking them in the Christian religion they take umbrage and avoid those churches where something more austere is demanded and offered. Or they form their own *cenacles* and elaborate their own cults where trite poetizings or unashamed heart throbs or tenuously masked passion itself may with some success pretend to fulfill the role of faith and its utter venture as it wrestles with God.

We need to be aware of the high price of religious faith, and not confuse it with the various aspects and talents of the inner life available to all comers. The analogy of poetry warns us that sentiments, emotions, memories, are but raw ingredients. Sentiments must be proved in life, "experiences" must be digested, emotions and memories must fade and again come to life in character. Then, perhaps, by an unrecognized gestation, a richer and deeper self having taken form, a true prayer may voice itself within us. Under favoring conditions a veil may suddenly be torn aside disclosing the true nature of our human situation and an impulse toward the love of our fellow creatures arise too majestic to dissipate, as do our common benevolences, under the tests of life. Unless some such maturing has taken place, some such price be paid, we are not in a position to recognize the signs and works and wonders of grace or to read with understanding the special rhetoric of faith as we find it in the Scriptures.

All this means selection, rejection, isolation, conflict for the believer as for the artist. The most elementary of all rules here—peculiarly offensive to the standing mores of our democratic outlook, where the truth that one man is as good as another is extended to condone mediocrity and to isolate and handicap excellence—this most elementary of all rules is that "a man must break with the existing order of the world and with its interests and values." This demand, which is a truism for the genuine artist, only echoes with varying depths of context the peremptory summons of Jesus to his disciples that found such frequent utterance: *"Go, sell whatsoever thou hast. . . ," "Seek first the kingdom of God and his righteousness."* And the new sphere, not of indemnification but rather of surpassingly lavish surpluses of discovery and satisfaction opened up, here and now in this age, is similarly indicated in the special symbols of the time:

There is no man that hath left house, or brethren, or sisters, or father, or mother, or wife, or children, or lands, for my sake, and for the gospel's, but he shall receive an hundredfold now in this time, houses, and brethren, and sisters, and mothers, and children, and lands, with persecutions.[2]

The analogy of the artist suggests, indeed, both the cost and the rewards of real devotion. For though, on the one hand, he makes himself as it were an Ishmaelite and a eunuch among men through the single-mindedness and intensity with which he pursues a special province among life's many offerings; on the other hand, he achieves a sensibility and a wealth and mastery in that province incommensurate with the common experience. He slowly builds up an unseen edifice of sensibility, a coral reef in the soul of significances and relationships, a house not made with hands of images and imaginings—an edifice wrought, indeed, out of the common realities, but set in new relations, bathed in the light of the imagination, transfigured not into a false unreality but into their true significance. Thus what began with the daily dust of life and the precisely observed fact of time and sense is now recognized to be a city let down from heaven.

If such a harvest after such a sowing—whether

of the artist or the Christian—appears strange, difficult, profitless to the man who has taken few steps outside the beaten path, or who has denied himself little, it is not a matter for surprise. These compensations are for the resolute and the reckless. There are those who sally forth toward discovery and achievement, but who, nevertheless, are careful to keep their communications with their base. Their life as men or artists is made up of a shuttling back and forth between the secure and the hazardous. They are commuters between the old and the new, between the sown land and the frontier. The new perspectives are not firmly grasped. But to enter into the new horizons calls for a decisiveness of repudiation and relinquishment, for a certain strain of grimness. Yet out of the grimness arises a greater joy, as "out of the strong came forth sweetness."

A modern poet has well stated the fateful hesitation, the clinging to wonted images, which prevent us from taking the dive into a more significant life. The parable is specially apt for a time of cultural crisis like our own where old securities, whether of faith or "way of life," are undermined. We may prefix to the poem the remark of Rilke: "They would so love to dwell among the signs and meanings that have become precious to them." C. Day

Lewis, in the poem, "Questions," shows us how easily we let ourselves be "immobilized" by present seductions which we nevertheless recognize for what they are.

How long will you keep this pose of self-
    confessed
And aspen hesitation
Dithering on the brink, obsessed
Immobilized by the feminine fascination
Of an image all your own,
Or doubting which is shadow, which is bone?

Will you wait womanish, while the flattering
    stream
Glosses your faults away?
Or would you find within that dream
Courage to break the dream, wisdom to say
That wisdom is not there?
Or is it simply the first shock you fear?

Do you need the horn in your ear, the hounds
    at your heel,
Gadflies to sting you sore,
The lightning's angry feint, and all
The horizon clouds boiling like lead, before
You'll risk your javelin dive
And pierce reflection's heart, and come alive?[3]

There is one further analogy in the work of the artist, particularly of the modern artist, that is worthy of attention here. We may illustrate by the foregoing poem. Reality, we have intimated, whether via art or faith is not easy of attainment; it is difficult. This difficulty inheres also inevitably in the language of genuine art and faith. It is always difficult for us to come alive to that which is beyond us, because it involves death in some measure. The language and symbols of that which is beyond us or new to us are strange until we have lived the new experience, the new relations. If we find the words of Shakespeare or the Bible clear, it is often because we short-cut and shortchange the sense; though to the degree that we have lived the experience and outlook in question we have insight.

The modern arts are difficult because they proceed out of the changed sensibility and experience of our time. The special images, subtleties, and concern of a modern poem like the one quoted above belong to the modern consciousness, and the significance of the poem is open only to those who have known something of the costs involved in the changing moral and psychological patterns of our day. The difficulty of the best modern art is the difficulty of the observer not of the artist. If the

observer or reader has not evaded the modern
spiritual situation, or lived on its margin, if he has
been responsibly concerned with the deeper di-
lemmas and anguish, public and intimate, of our
century and has had some interest in and understanding of the nature of art, he will find that the
modern poet or artist speaks to him.

But here we have an analogy of the far richer
complex of the Christian consciousness and its
grammar and thesaurus. Faith has its own rhetoric,
and spiritual things are not only spiritually dis-
cerned but are reported in a spiritual tongue. This
is not to draw a fixed line between spirit and flesh,
or between supernatural and natural. For all that is
spiritual is first and indeed always in a sense natural. The language of faith may, however, be difficult and strange because we have not lived through
the costs that illuminate it. It is a question of where
we live and of our standpoint. The artist has paid
his price and offers his vision of the world to those
who have to some degree followed him. The modern
artist of our world under judgment has exposed his
nerves and heart to the fury and desolation of these
decades, and can provide meaning for those who
have the same initiation. To those who come to the
gospel and the Scriptures, not with a wealth of

sentiments or a success story of immunities achieved but with a heart exercised in responsibilities, the veiled symbols of vocation and promise will be as their native tongue.

FOOTNOTES

1. Paris: Editions Emile-Paul Frères, 1926, pp. 25-26.

2. Mark 10:30.

3. "Questions" from *Short Is the Time* by C. Day Lewis. Copyright 1940, 1943 by Oxford University Press, Inc. Reprinted by permission.

Kenneth W. Thompson

PROPHETS AND POLITICS

Walter Lippmann in *The Public Philosophy* grapples
with an issue that has long concerned Reinhold
Niebuhr in lectures and writings, namely, the problem of a relevant political ethic. There are, Mr.
Lippmann argues, two realms that earlier and wiser
philosophers and theologians described as the kingdom of God and the kingdom of man. The one is the
realm of the spirit; the other is a realm of immediate, particular, and ambiguous events. He doubts
that the wisdom of one can serve the other, for there
is a hiatus between religious and philosophic truths
and the actual perplexities with which man must
deal. In a day when religious prophets and secular
high priests often proclaim that political problems
would quickly be swept aside if leaders trusted
more to their common humanity, Mr. Lippmann
shockingly asserts that modern-day seers and saints
have remarkably little to offer by way of practical
advice and specific guidance. For those who look
to eternal verities for directly applicable political

solutions, he observes: "The deposit of wisdom in the Bible and in the classic books does not contain a systematic and comprehensive statement of moral principles from which it is possible to deduce with clarity and certainty specific answers to concrete questions." In consequence, men look to religion in vain for tidy, comprehensive, or deducible answers to specific current problems.

This view is patently a heresy if we hold it up to recent official pronouncements of Catholic and Protestant leaders. One highly placed churchman writes that the Evanston Report on International Affairs which "asserts the Christian imperatives of action for peace" certainly "provides relevant guidance for . . . the years immediately ahead."[1] Another far bolder declaration of November 20, 1954, by the Administrative Board of the Catholic Welfare Conference implies that the godly righteous who have renounced atheistic materialism will be able "to withstand the enemy from without." The Catholic hierarchy concludes that the godly righteous in the name of the Cross can triumph over the new paganism of godless sinners expressed in secularism in politics and avarice in business and the professions. A third and more recent Protestant pronouncement is found in this statement: "As for the relation of church agencies to the program of technical co-operation it will suffice to say that in so far as this program is essentially humanitarian in character, Christian missionaries and the personnel of church-related institutions are prepared and eager to co-operate with this program, on a consultative and voluntary basis."[2] The balance of the text invites us to infer that unless the church can impose its own humanitarian terms on the enterprise of states, it will eschew co-operation.

If Mr. Lippmann's views are alien to present-day religious thought, it must be said that the distillate of these three pronouncements taken together comprises a political ethic that bears almost no relationship to the thought of devout and learned minds through the ages. At the same time it spurns the honest secular wisdom compressed in Mr. Lippmann's little book; it has no more in common with Augustine than with Niebuhr. It seems bereft of the deepest Reformation insight placing us all, whether sinners or saints, under the same condemnation in the city of this world where "there is a law in their members which wars against the law that is in their minds." For moderns, the prevailing and official approach to the relation of church and state, whether Catholic or Protestant, is more buoyantly optimistic about the translation of objective religious truths into concrete political policies than about the theory of the two realms. The historic view insists that although no definitive demarcation line can be drawn between the two orbits, the texture of one is existence and of the other, spirit. The relation between the imperatives of religion and politics is a never-ending problem for inquiry in each contingent circumstance. Religion is at one and the same time irrelevant as a sure guide to the perplexities of practice and eternally relevant as ultimate transcendent principle. The assumptions and consequences of the historic and modern approaches are in this sense fundamentally at odds with one another. In no sphere is the choice of one or the other conception of political ethics more fraught with consequences than in international relations, for the answer to the query whether ethics have any bearing at all upon international politics rests with the formulation of a more relevant concept of ethics. When a particular version of international morality is found wanting in practice, publicists, philosophers, and politicians conclude that morality has nothing to do with politics. This happens to be a rough and approximate account for international politics of the temper of our present era. Wilsonian morality which equated peace and a good international society with democracy and national self-determination was rather too simple to meet the harsh necessities, for example, of a viable economy in Central Europe. Even great men —or perhaps especially great men—join, without knowing it, the procession Burckhardt called "the terrible simplifiers." If there is an absolute in the realm of political ethics, it is that no single proximate moral standard, whether self-determination or the United Nations, can be held up as an absolute.

This is at the root of our modern predicament as a current example will illustrate. The halls of Congress are perhaps not the most likely schoolroom for an examination of political ethics, and yet the pathos of our quest for a relevant political ethic was caught with clarity and perception by a staff member of the *New York Herald Tribune* who on February 22, 1955, reported on the statements of Mr. George V. Allen, former Ambassador to India and at this writing Assistant Secretary for Near Eastern Affairs, and of Mr. Van Kirk to the Subcommittee on Technical Assistance of the Senate Foreign Relations Committee. The former ambassador cast his argument for technical assistance to countries like India in essentially political terms.

It was in our interest to prevent India from turning for aid and comfort to the Communists. If we would avoid the stigma of hypocrisy, we should not conceal the fact that the imperatives of our national existence command us to lend what assistance we can to this pivotal Asian member of the British Commonwealth. If we are less forthright, we shall only invite the resentment, disdain, and rebuke of the Indians, who will point to the dross of self-interest that joins inextricably with the gold of moral purpose in every foreign policy. The best we can do, Mr. Allen advises, is to identify and consolidate our interests with those of India. Indeed, the highest ethical standard for nations may be the mutuality of their national interests and purposes. India, with a subcontinent to exploit and develop, shares with us the need of an era of economic growth, international peace, and security. Thus it must be said that the relevant political ethic for the diplomatist requires, to begin with, an awareness that the texture of interstate relations is comprised of multiple national interests, with their military, political, economic, and moral components, which clash in conflict or are resolved in consensus and agreement. In politics, interest or power and morality can rarely be conceived of in isolation; and ethical judgments must be made not in the abstract but in relation to the contingent realities of the particular situation. Moral principles in their pure form seldom intrude on the political but are modified in the light of the facts of interest and power.

Dr. Van Kirk, on the other hand, prefers to believe that good policies can be free of any such ambiguity and uncertainty. The issue of right and wrong is unequivocal and unmistakable. If government policies result in programs that "are essentially humanitarian in character," the churches will give their support. "It is important . . . that programs of technical co-operation be kept wholly independent of considerations of military or defense strategy." He contends that "the U. S. Technical Co-operation Program is sufficiently important and effective to stand on its merits and is therefore fully justified without reference to military or defense support objectives." In these terms the art of governing is the quest for broad humanitarian objectives, not the search for practical national objectives that serve both the state and its friends.

The crux of the problem confronting us emerges in the juxtaposition of these two points of view. On the one hand, the diplomat who proceeds within the narrow limits of the national interest is unlikely to conceive of principles or programs divorced from the necessities of the state. On the other hand, the churchman transcends the turmoil of politics as such. The statesman's first duty is to the people, or "generations living and dead," whose safety and welfare he is pledged to protect and defend. If acts of generosity and magnanimity endanger national security, he cannot but turn his back. In the same spirit he looks to responsible leaders of other states as, first and foremost, their peoples' guardians. Recognizing the paramountcy of the national interest for those he represents abroad, he can hardly be surprised to find others subject to the same standards and considerations. With moderation and wisdom he may be enabled to discover the points at which his national interest and theirs come together, not primarily in abstract pronouncements but in the daily search for consensus on specific issues and policies. Technical assistance, no less than military assistance, must be viewed in this context; and it will not do to say that what is done in one sphere has no bearing or dependence upon what is done in the other. Both are grounded in the mutual self-interest of the participating powers and the convergence of their needs and interests at the nodal points where policies are worked out. For, as the West's experience in Asia attests, there must first be created a viable economic base before programs of military assistance can be expected to succeed. Likewise, economic reform in the absence of military security can only tempt the lurking aggressor. It is significant that India, which more than any Asian country has emphasized the primacy of economic over military aid, was among the first, through its ambassador, to commend American policy makers for the firm stand taken in 1950 in Korea. This, the Indians were convinced, was an earnest of our decision not to scuttle Asia; it was the indispensable prerequisite for programs of social and economic reform on which, with our help, others hoped to embark.

It can, of course, be argued that local and particular interests are absorbed and disappear within the programs of the United Nations. This, in fact, is the prevailing view of moderns who insist that foreign policies must be humanitarian in character. In all this we are reminded of research trends in the 1930's in international studies when American scholars preferred to view every international movement as good, and all national efforts as bad. Where the League of Nations and National Socialism were concerned, this distinction was in general quite plausible. If the examples had been the Communist International and the legitimate aspirations for national security of, say, England or the United States, the dichotomy between good internationalism and bad nationalism would have been seen to be fallacious. Indeed, scholars since the war have conceived of international institutions essentially in terms of international politics, which is to say, they have studied the United Nations in terms of the respective claims for national security by the member states. International organizations provide the framework within which nations strive to harmonize their independent purposes, and United Nations policies are essentially the resultant of the policies of its members.

The same prophets who urge that defense and security objectives must be wholly disassociated from technical assistance are, however, inclined to conceive of the United Nations as *deus ex machina*. They seem to believe that if states in their practice are often self-consciously defensive and militaristic, the new international machinery will rid them of this archaism of an earlier, more evil age. Moreover, since the good life is associated with broad humanitarian objectives contrasted with narrow nationalistic aims, a program by the United Nations is by definition superior to one carried forward on unilateral or regional terms. It so happens in Asia and Africa where the memory of Western imperialism is strong, that a multilateral U.N. program of technical assistance based on genuine international consensus and executed by multiracial personnel is more likely to be well received. Yet the risk of too absolute a commitment in politics is illustrated on precisely this point. Recognized authorities tell us that in some parts of the world, for example, at some places in Latin America, U.S. personnel have been more acceptable and effective than U.N. personnel, and in Asia the prestige of the Colombo Plan has often been very great. Moreover, it is sometimes argued that the number of autonomous agencies, whether national or international, in the technical assistance field together often fail to do justice to the magnitude of their task.

Mr. Lippmann is therefore right in at least three respects when he questions the relevance of religion for politics. First, the religious point of view which provides so-called humanitarian goals for the statesman as a direct and immediate substitute for selfish national purposes "misconceives the nature of international relations." It assumes that states, even more than individuals, are capable of pure altruism, whereas precisely the opposite is the case. Second, it falsely presumes that the components of foreign policy are easily separable and that what we do in the economic sphere need have nothing to do with our military aims. Since the various facets of our policy—economic, psychological, military and political—are all grounded in the same objective considerations of national interest and seldom susceptible for long to the whimsy or good will of a President or Secretary of State, this distinction is likewise defective. Third, and most basic, religion is so consistently irrelevant to politics because the problem of the translation of ideas from one modality to another is often obscured. Religion, like philosophy, assumes that objective and ultimate truths, as such, are absolute in character. Yet absolute truth in politics is singularly inappropriate. Moreover, religious observers and publicists create for themselves pseudoreligious absolutes out of political machinery and programs that are more wisely and effectively viewed in pragmatic terms by the diplomatist.

Religion, in short, is resistant to successful foreign policy when the city of man is equated with the city of God. More properly conceived, it offers resources for understanding the nature of man and politics. Christian realism, by illuminating the misery and grandeur of man, can be a textbook for the diplomatist. It can rid men of their illusions while preparing them for their "finest hours." But more important for our purposes, Chrstian realism provides proximate moral standards that are neither as lofty as "the law of love" nor as bitterly tragic as the struggle for power. I take it that Christian realism accepts the fact and reality of the two realms but dedicates itself untiringly to an inquiry into political behavior at the boundary line separating the two. If there is an answer to Mr. Lippmann—and to some extent he corroborates this himself—it lies not in official religious pronouncement but in the philosophy that informs *Christianity and Crisis*. Incidentally, the quality of mind and character of this journal's senior editor, Reinhold Niebuhr, that makes the deepest imprint on younger followers is the contempt he shares with John Milton for "a fugitive and cloistered virtue, unexercised and unbreathed, that never sallies out and sees her adversary, but slinks out of the race where that immortal garland is to be run for, not without dust and heat."

FOOTNOTES

1. *Christianity and Crisis*, Vol. XIV, No. 22, p. 176.
2. Statement by Mr. Walter W. Van Kirk, Executive Director of the Department of International Affairs of the National Council of Churches, to the Subcommittee on Technical Assistance Programs of the Senate Committee on Foreign Relations, February 21, 1955.

Reinhold Niebuhr

RELIGIOSITY AND THE
CHRISTIAN FAITH

A visitor to our shores would probably come to the same conclusion at which St. Paul arrived in regard to the Athenians, namely, that we are "very religious." But the judgment might not imply a compliment any more than Paul wanted to so imply when he called attention to the worship of many gods in Athens, including the "unknown god." Our religiosity seems to have as little to do with the Christian faith as the religiosity of the Athenians.

The "unknown god" in America seems to be faith itself. Our politicians are always admonishing the people to have "faith." Sometimes they seem to imply that faith is in itself redemptive. Sometimes this faith implies faith in something. That something is usually an idol, rather than the "God and father of our Lord Jesus Christ," who both judges and has mercy upon sinful men and nations. Sometimes we are asked to have faith in ourselves, sometimes to have faith in humanity, sometimes to have faith in America. Sometimes it is hope, rather than faith, which is really intended. We are to have hope that we will win the "cold war" or that the "cold war" will not break out into an atomic conflict.

These provisional hopes are no doubt rather better than despair, for desperate actions and policies are generated in despair. But the objects of faith are almost always idolatrous. For whether it is in ourselves, or in mankind, or in civilization, or in America, that we are asked to have faith, the admonition always points to an object of faith which is less than God and which certainly does not deserve unreserved commitment or adoration. The question is whether a generation which has lost its faith in all the gods of the nineteenth century, that is, in "history," or "progress," or "enlightenment," or the "perfectibility of man," is not expressing its desire to believe in something, to be committed somehow, even though it is not willing to be committed to a God who can be known only through repentance, and whose majesty judges all human pretensions. It is precisely faith in this God which is avoided in all this religiosity. A nation as powerful and as fortunate as ours is not inclined to wor-

ship a God before whom "the nations are as a drop
in the bucket," and "who bringeth princes to
naught." Our modern religiosity, in short, expresses
various forms of self-worship. It is a more specifical-
ly religious ethos than the so-called "secular" faiths
which history in our tragic age has refuted. The
strategy seems to be to bring the discredited pagan
gods in Christian disguises, hoping that the traditional piety may be merged with the secular forms
of self-confidence.

The cause of this procedure seems to be that we
are so sure of ourselves, of our power and of our
virtue, and yet we are not sure of our destiny at all.
We live on the edge of an abyss, and at any moment
our private securities may be swallowed in the
world-wide insecurity. The religiosity which seems
to correspond to this combination of self-esteem and
anxiety would seem to be a secular faith clothed in
traditional terms. The most disquieting aspect of
such religiosity is that it is frequently advanced by
popular leaders of the Christian church and is not
regarded as a substitute, but as an interpretation of
that faith. The gospel admonition, "Repent ye, for
the kingdom of heaven is at hand," is a challenge to
submit all our achievements and ambitions and
hopes to a much higher judge than those judges

who support our self-esteem. This admonition would seem to have little affinity with the "power of positive thinking."

It is significant that although this modern religiosity makes for self-esteem, particularly collective self-esteem, the nation is helped to find and to hold its rightful place in the perilous position of leadership in the alliance of free nations by many shrewd and critical "secular" thinkers who help us to weigh our responsibilities and judge the hazards of the task in which we are engaged. One must come to the conclusion that religion *per se* and faith *per se* are not virtuous, or a cause of virtue. The question is always what the object of worship is, and whether the worship tends to break the pride of the self so that a truer self may arise, either individually or collectively. If worship and faith do not serve this rebirth of men and of nations they are the source of confusion. We can therefore take no satisfaction in the pervasive religiosity of our nation. Much of it is a perversion of the Christian gospel. It aggravates, rather than mitigates, the problems of a very successful people.

It will be remembered that the prophet Jeremiah was worried about the false prophets who did not speak "the word of the Lord" but spoke their own dreams and imaginations. He had a test for detecting false prophecy. The false prophet was one who accentuated complacency and promised those who despised God, "You shall have assured peace in this place." It is as difficult in our day as in the day of Jeremiah to preach "the word of the Lord," for that runs counter to the complacency of men and of nations. It is sharper than a "two-edged sword." It must hurt before it can heal.